HOW TO BUILD A BETTER MOUSETRAP CAR
—and Other Experimental Science Fun

HOW TO BUILD A BETTER MOUSETRAP CAR
—and Other Experimental Science Fun

Written and illustrated by
AL G. RENNER

DODD, MEAD & COMPANY
New York

Library of Congress Cataloging in Publication Data

Renner, Al G.
    How to build a better mousetrap car—and other
experimental science fun.

    Includes index.
    SUMMARY: Science experiments using such
models as mousetrap cars, paper plate Frisbees,
toothpick bridges, and milk carton windmills which
the experimenter makes himself and then changes
and rebuilds as he tests scientific data.
    1. Science—Experiments—Juvenile literature.
2. Models and modelmaking—Juvenile literature.
3. Experimental design—Juvenile literature.
[1. Science—Experiments. 2. Models and
modelmaking. 3. Experimental design] I. Title.
Q164.R46   500.2'028   76-48912
ISBN 0-396-07419-7

CONTENTS

THIS BOOK IS YOUR INVITATION TO
EXPERIMENTAL FUN. IT WAS DESIGNED
TO DEVELOP YOUR MODEL BUILDING
CREATIVITY. YOU WILL DESIGN YOUR
OWN MODELS ONLY TO CHANGE THEM
EXPERIMENTALLY AGAIN AND AGAIN.

DO NOT EXPECT ANY RECIPE-TYPE
INSTRUCTIONS; THERE WILL BE NO
MEASUREMENTS TO FOLLOW; YOU WILL
NOT BE ASKED TO BUY SPECIFIC MATER-
IALS. YOU WILL BE ENCOURAGED TO
CREATE YOUR OWN DESIGNS.

YOU SHOULD BE FOREWARNED,
HOWEVER, THAT EXPERIMENTAL FUN
PROBLEMS LIKE THESE ONLY LEAD TO
MORE INTERESTING PROBLEMS TO
INVESTIGATE. YOU MIGHT EVEN FIND
YOURSELF BUILDING MENTAL MODELS
IN YOUR SLEEP.

CHAPTER ONE

HOW TO HAVE EXPERIMENTAL FUN

CHANGE THINGS!

CAN YOU?

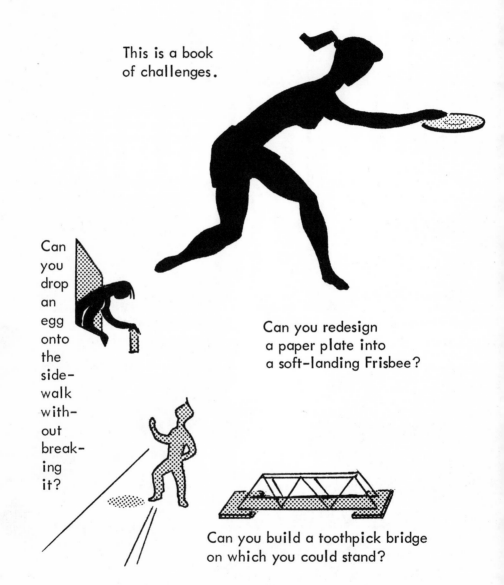

This is a book
of challenges.

Can
you
drop
an
egg
onto
the
side-
walk
with-
out
break-
ing
it?

Can you redesign
a paper plate into
a soft-landing Frisbee?

Can you build a toothpick bridge
on which you could stand?

CAN YOU?

Can you start a fire by
rubbing two sticks together?

Can you make a milk carton
windmill do useful work?

Can you make a
model racing car
run just on mouse-
trap power?

It sure is
fun to try. You
will be surprised
when you can do most
of these things. Experi-
mental fun can lead you in
many directions. You will
have to pick and choose
what is of most interest to you.

BUILD A MODEL TO REBUILD IT

This book encourages you to build a model only to change it and rebuild it again and again to improve it. You are invited first to build a mousetrap car. This car is easy to build; yet there is much to learn from it about levers and pulleys and their relationships. The learning is in the changing, the experimenting and the rebuilding, and not in a quickly finished model.

You can build your mousetrap car just for fun, to compete with other neighborhood experimenters, or to challenge your science class at school to build a better car. You can organize your own Mousetrap "500."

Experiment with many variations of your model car. Invent new parts and try the inventions of your friends. Design a new kind of racing car. Then combine all of the very best materials and conditions which you have found into a super car for the Mousetrap "500."

When this experimental procedure is used by a group such as a Scout troop, a club, or a science class, learning is exciting as new data is generated and as new ideas are tested by rival experimenters and inventors. Competition can become very keen as the frontiers of knowledge are expanded.

Experimenting can get you in trouble, though, if it leaves a mess around your room or on your work table at school. The next few pages will suggest ways of getting materials for experimenting and how to organize them so that your family and your friends can enjoy your experimenting as much as you will.

Most of the materials which are suggested for experimental fun in this book are disposable items which will cost you nothing. Get a brown paper market bag and place it where your family can drop in materials for you. Tell them of your needs so that they can do more for you. Then make other ecology bags for your neighbors and relatives.

You will find many surprises in your ecology bags which you can transfer to your organizer. Here is a starter list of things which you can request:

Milk cartons

Foam egg cartons

Foam cups

Spools

Thread

String

Cord

Wire

Paper plates

Ice cream sticks

Coffee stir sticks

Soda straws

Stub candles

Jar tops

Plastic covers

Plastic bags

Rubber bands

Paper clips

Corks

Nails

Screws

Bolts and nuts

Organize your tools and equipment in a cardboard box that you can get out and put away easily into a cupboard or into a clothes closet. You will get to do much more experimenting if your tools and materials are always ready.

The labels on the milk carton filing boxes shown above are only suggested. Make these filing boxes fit your own needs. The extra space which is often found at the end of the box can hold school binders, folders, books, or your laboratory records. You will find yourself to be a much more popular experimenter if your tools and materials are always put away.

BUILD AN ORGANIZER

The filing boxes for your organizer are made from paper milk cartons. These strong boxes are most easily cut with a slanted razor blade, but any sharp cutting instrument will serve well.

The most important feature of this filing box for your organizer is the one-centimeter rim which is left around the opening of the box. This rim eliminates the need for shelves which must be sawed and nailed. These filing boxes slide over each other very conveniently on this rim.

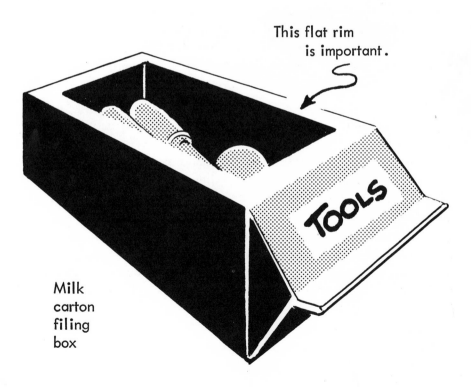

This flat rim is important.

Milk carton filing box

HAVE EXPERIMENTAL FUN

Science is a most enjoyable subject to study because you get to develop ideas as well as to talk and to write about them. Theories need experimental proof, and this comes from exciting work in the laboratory. Your own laboratory can be your work desk at home.

Experimenting is simply changing something purposely to learn more about it, and this is fun. We get tired of looking at the same thing after a while. Being able to change something often opens a new approach to the problem.

Watch for conditions and properties which make a difference. When you can make that difference happen over and over again, you are beginning to have control over an event. This should make you feel good. Often, even without knowing it, you are beginning to understand the problem. Be sure to look for hidden differences.

A condition is a state of being. The wheels for your mousetrap car can be smaller-larger, narrower-wider, smoother-rougher, lighter-heavier, and even duller-brighter. These are just a few of the conditional things about wheels which can be changed in your experimenting.

Properties are the characteristic attributes of objects and materials. They cannot be changed because they give identity; however, you can always substitute new objects and materials into the experiment which should introduce new properties.

CHAPTER TWO

MOUSETRAP CARS

CAN YOU MAKE A MOUSETRAP POWERED CAR GO FARTHEST?

QUICK START CAR

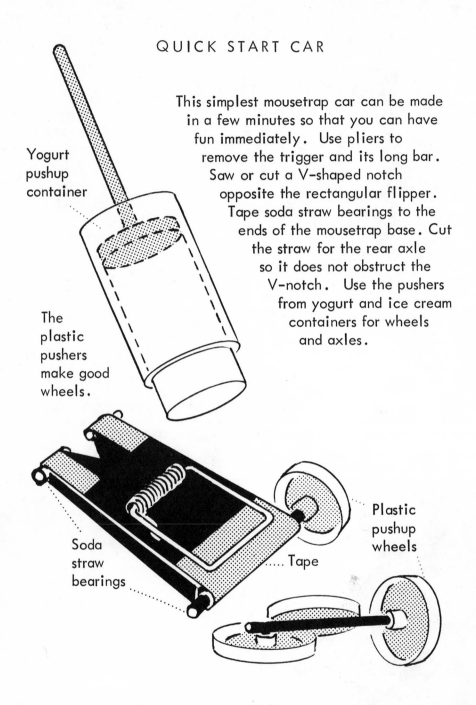

Yogurt
pushup
container

The
plastic
pushers
make good
wheels.

This simplest mousetrap car can be made in a few minutes so that you can have fun immediately. Use pliers to remove the trigger and its long bar. Saw or cut a V-shaped notch opposite the rectangular flipper. Tape soda straw bearings to the ends of the mousetrap base. Cut the straw for the rear axle so it does not obstruct the V-notch. Use the pushers from yogurt and ice cream containers for wheels and axles.

Soda
straw
bearings

Tape

Plastic
pushup
wheels

QUICK START CAR

Tie and glue a string to the rear axle. When the glue is dry, wind some of the string on the axle. Pull the string to make the rear wheels spin. Why couldn't mousetrap power make the wheels spin for you? Tie the loose end of the string to the rectangular flipper. Cock the spring with the flipper and wind the string onto the rear axle again.

When you put this car on the floor to let it go, be ready to get out of the way! The quick start car has power for a short distance, and it may waste that power just spinning its wheels if the floor is smooth. After a little experimenting you should be able to convert this power to speed and distance.

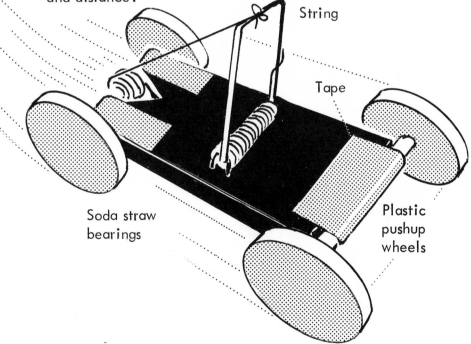

String

Tape

Soda straw bearings

Plastic pushup wheels

PUSH OFF CAR

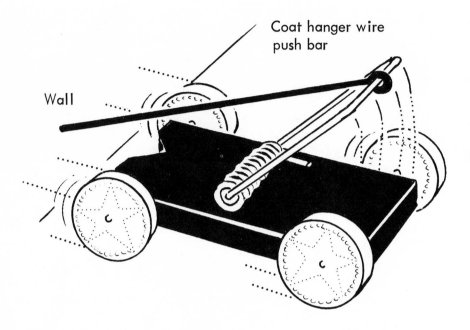

Coat hanger wire
push bar

Wall

This is another easy-to-make car which will help you to get started. Tack four checkers to the mousetrap base for wheels. A hot small nail will melt holes through plastic checkers quickly. Fasten a section of coat hanger wire to the flipper to be used as a push bar.

Would a lighter or a heavier car coast farther? Try and see. Make your cars build up as much momentum as possible. Momentum is the accumulated potential energy which is stored in a moving car and which keeps it moving after its power has been used.

CATAPULT CAR

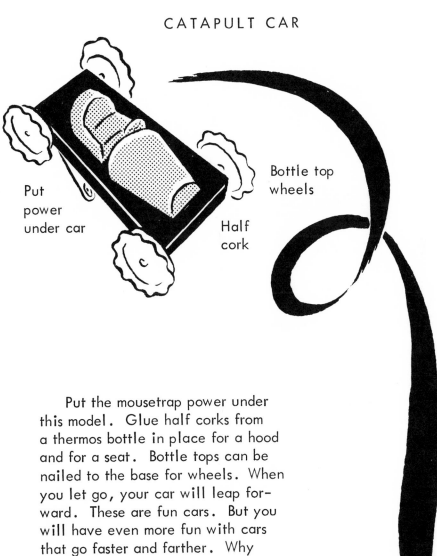

Put
power
under car

Bottle top
wheels

Half
cork

Put the mousetrap power under
this model. Glue half corks from
a thermos bottle in place for a hood
and for a seat. Bottle tops can be
nailed to the base for wheels. When
you let go, your car will leap for-
ward. These are fun cars. But you
will have even more fun with cars
that go faster and farther. Why
don't you start experimenting now
with these three cars and others to
get all of the very best features on
one super car?

CHANGE THE WHEELS

Now is the time to start experimenting. Change something to learn more about these cars. Let us start by changing the wheels. Keep watching for the best combination of the conditions and the properties.

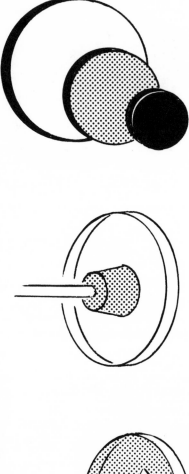

There is a full range of jar and bottle tops available for wheels. Vial caps are the smallest, and paint can lids are the largest.

Make the hole for the axle with a nail or with a drill. You may need a cork hub to steady the wheel. Tape can be used, too, to steady wheels.

If you would like to solder a metal bottle cap to a coat hanger wire axle, the metal must be hot, clean, bare, and bright.

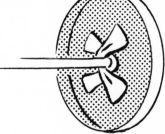

Axle bearings should be as frictionless as possible; but you will want tires that grip the wooden floor securely with the greatest amount of friction.

Pour the sand over fresh glue on the wheels or bury the glued wheels in sand.

Stretching a wide rubber band around a wheel makes a fine tire. Many different sizes of rubber bands are available at stationery stores. Small, colorful balloon sections can be cut and stretched around the wheels.

Several layers of rubber cement can work as well as rubber bands or balloons. Remember that your car will be losing energy if your wheels slip.

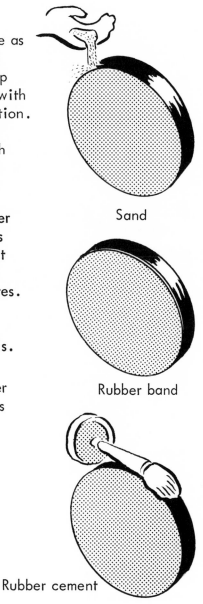

Sand

Rubber band

Rubber cement

CHANGE THE WHEELS

Plastic container covers make fine wheels when you want your car to be lightweight. Always look for the center mark on the cover when making the hole for the axle. This hole can be made most easily by melting it through with a hot nail. Hold the nail with a cloth or with a paper towel which has been wrapped around it. Or you can hold the nail with pliers.

CHANGE THE WHEELS

Don't overlook the fact that spools can be used as wheels as well as corks, checkers, broom handle sections, buttons, and tubular containers such as medicinal vials. These are often used for front wheels.

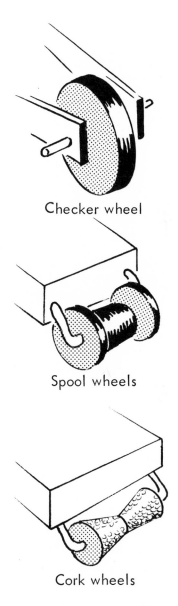

Checker wheel

Coat hanger wire which has been bent into a U-shape is a good axle to support the front wheels on a wood car body. Such a small axle often requires a tube bearing and a tape bushing to fit the large holes of spools and other improvised wheels.

Spool wheels

A loose bearing is often a source of friction and vibration. This is a common source of energy loss in these small cars.

Cork wheels

CHANGE THE AXLES

Should the rear axle pulley be large or small? You can decide this best when you experiment with the other conditions which will exist with it.

Wire axle pulley

Remember that a pulley is a form of lever. You have wound the string on the plastic axle of the quick start car. That was a very small pulley. You can use a spool for a larger, rear axle pulley, and you can use a fishing line reel or a typewriter reel for a still larger pulley if you make the body of your car a little longer.

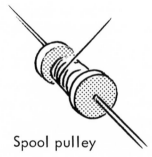

Spool pulley

Pulleys are levers which can give you speed or power. Which do you want for your model?

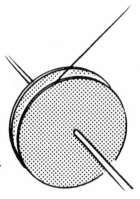

Fishing reel pulley

CHANGE THE AXLES

Good axles can be made from pencils, pens, rods, dowels, soda straws, tubes, wires, nails and bolts. Pins and screws are used sometimes, too.

If your wheels wobble, you need bearings to keep them straight and free of friction. The simplest bearings can be plastic soda straws which are taped to the wheels on both sides. Copper, brass, and aluminum tubing make sturdier bearings, but a hacksaw is needed for cutting them.

Sometimes a bearing does not fit the wheel hole. Wrapping the bearing with a bushing of masking tape will make it fit any hole. Narrow cardboard, paper, and can lid wheels usually have bad wobble problems. A bearing made from a checker, a dowel section, or a cork can be glued to the side of the wheel to make the hub wider and more stable.

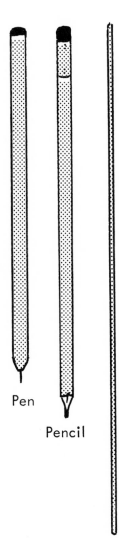

Pen

Pencil

Coat hanger wire

Milk cartons and other boxes can be cut flat for bodies. Milk carton paper is extremely strong, plasticized paper which is easily cut with a slanted razor blade. Use a paper punch or a sharp pencil point to make axle holes.

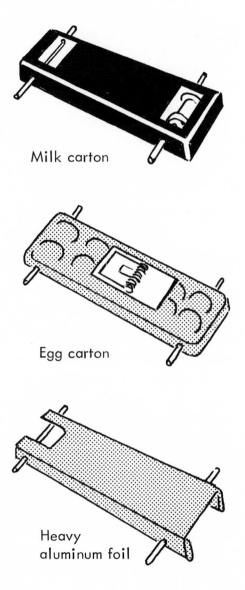

Milk carton

If you desire a very lightweight car body, an egg carton or its top will serve well. Plastic sponges have been used, too, because of their lightness. They are easy to drill and to shape. Polyurethane foam is always an ideal model material.

Egg carton

Thin sheet metal such as in aluminum plates is a fine body material when bent into an inverted U-shape. Bend the edges double for strength.

Heavy
aluminum foil

26

CHANGE THE BODY

The mousetrap is
a car body in itself if
you fasten the wheels
and axles to the base
as was shown on the
first three cars at the
beginning of this
chapter. However, you
can experiment more
with a body made of
wood or foam plastic.
Glue or nail the mouse-
trap to the block. You
can use eye bolts for the
front bearings, or you
can drill holes through
the body for axles.
Cut a notch at the back
of the car for the string
that turns the axle and
wheels.

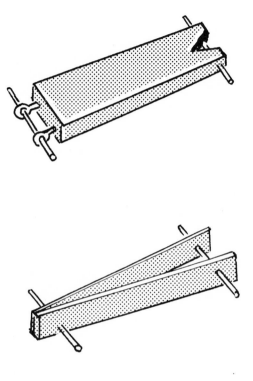

Two rulers on edge
can form a V-shaped
body frame, and do not
overlook the possibilities
of a single ruler on edge
for a body. A section
of broom handle serves
well, too.

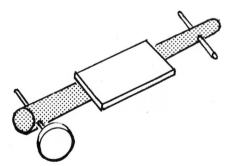

Would a shorter lever or a longer lever work better as a flipper? Do you want speed, power, or distance?

It is easy to shorten the flipper lever. Some common ways to lengthen the flipper are shown here because this is harder to do.

A coat hanger wire works best as a flipper lever when it is doubled to make it stronger. It can be tied or taped to the flipper.

A ruler makes a handy wooden or plastic extension. Should this lever be shorter or longer? Should it be lighter or heavier? You can find what works best in your combination of conditions by experimenting.

Coat hanger wire

Coat hanger wire

Wooden ruler

28

CHANGE THE FLIPPER

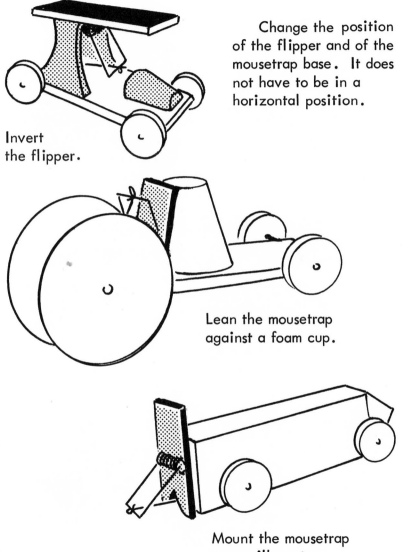

Change the position of the flipper and of the mousetrap base. It does not have to be in a horizontal position.

Invert the flipper.

Lean the mousetrap against a foam cup.

Mount the mousetrap on a milk carton.

CHANGE THE FLIPPER

Why not use a pulley instead of a flipper so that the spring can unwind all the way instead of just that half sweep which it has been traveling? How could you wind the spring even tighter than it was when you bought it?

You can quickly make a pulley of any size by gluing three cardboard circles together. The middle circle should be of a smaller diameter to form the groove of the pulley. Make a generous slot in the body for this larger pulley. Mount the pulley and the spring on a separate axle which can be made from coat hanger wire.

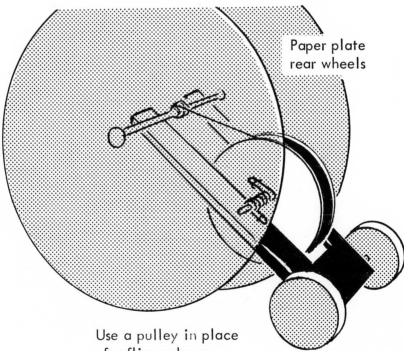

Paper plate
rear wheels

Use a pulley in place
of a flipper lever.

CHANGE THE FLIPPER

You could make the mousetrap base spin instead of the flipper. Fasten the inverted mousetrap under the axle. Now the mousetrap must unwind as the lever with little wheel presses against the floor. How could you make this flipper spin more than the normal half turn?

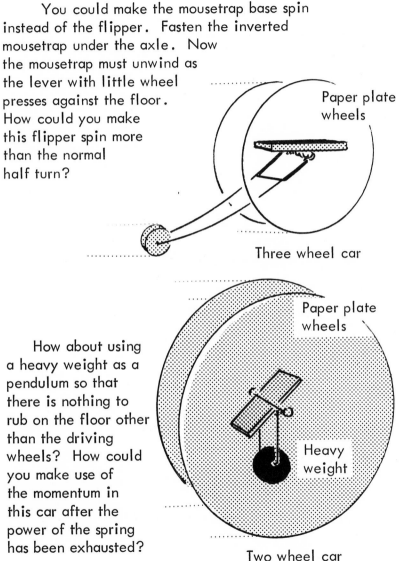

Paper plate wheels

Three wheel car

Paper plate wheels

How about using a heavy weight as a pendulum so that there is nothing to rub on the floor other than the driving wheels? How could you make use of the momentum in this car after the power of the spring has been exhausted?

Heavy weight

Two wheel car

KINDS OF COMPETITION

Competition can be a fine test of skills in the use of levers and pulleys. There can be individual and team entries in the following events:

SPEED. This is fun competition, but it is hard to judge because it is very hard to start a number of cars at the same time.

DISTANCE. This is the most popular and is the easiest to judge. Whose car can go farthest on one swing of the mousetrap flipper?

MOST ORIGINAL DESIGN. Encourage unusual designs even though they may not be practical. This could be a warm-up competition before the big event. A patent committee could honor new designs with patent certificates. New ideas could be shared for the improvement of all cars; however, it is important that credit always be given to the originator.

MOST POWERFUL. The cars must pull small trailers loaded with weights. The car moving the greatest weight for a designated distance is the winner. The big problem in this event is to get the driving wheels to maintain friction with the floor.

BEST DECORATED. Participants whose cars obviously will not be winners often like to decorate their racers just to make the event more colorful. A special award should encourage this noble effort.

SUGGESTED RULES FOR COMPETITION

Design your own rules for the best conditions under which to hold your Mousetrap "500." The rules on this page are here only to get you started.

1. Use standard mousetraps so that each entrant has the same fair chance. Occasionally entrants will want to use the larger rattraps. This would be fair if everyone had the same kind of trap.

2. Use improvised wheels only. Manufactured wheels can be quite expensive when purchased; however, it is much more inventive to make your own wheels.

3. No manufactured parts may be used other than the mousetrap. Occasionally experimenters want to use their own erector sets or mechanical kits. This is acceptable if there are enough parts to be shared with each member of the group. Every experimenter should have an equal opportunity to do his or her best. Much more ingenuity can be developed by improvising your own car parts.

Be sure to have an official starter with a checkered flag. This person can also serve as announcer. You may also need a timer and a measurer. Hold your Mousetrap "500" in a large room with a hardwood floor or in a gymnasium.

RACING CAR BIBLIOGRAPHY

After experimenting is a good time to read to get more data about racing cars. You will appreciate the information more. Look up automobiles and simple machines as well as racing cars. Look for key words like levers, pulleys, gears, gear ratios, machines, engines, motors, momentum, and transfer of energy.

The Book of Popular Science, 1976, Volume 3, pages 56-61

Compton's Encyclopedia, 1974, Volume 1, pages 784-818

Merit Students' Encyclopedia, 1976, Volume 1, pages 444-474

World Book Encyclopedia, 1976, Volume 1, pages 950-952

Del Valle	Cars on Road and Track
Edmonds	Hot Rodding for Beginners
Felson	Here Is Your Hobby
Jackson	Racing Cars
Schneider	Push, Pull and Lift
Sharp	Simple Machines and How They Work
Sootin	Experiments with Machines and Matter
Syrocki	What Is a Machine?

CHAPTER THREE

FRISBEES

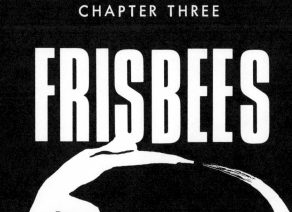

COULD YOU WIN
A PAPER PLATE
FRISBEE TOURNAMENT?

A Frisbee is such a simple device.
"A paper plate or a large plastic cover should
do the same thing," you say. However, they don't
until you make a few experimental changes.

The paper plate always turns over and skids in
for a landing on its bottom. "That is because it has
a dihedral shape," the paper airplane designers will
probably try to explain to you.

Could you redesign a paper plate into a real
Frisbee and enter it into an experimental fun Frisbee
tournament? This book will give you a chance to do
just that.

Experiment with the paper plate until you can
control the differences in its flight. Make it fade
to the left and to the right. Try to make it fly
straight to the target. Even make it come back to you
like a boomerang. Be sure that you can make it coast
in for a soft landing.

CHANGE THE SIZE

There are not as many objects in the experimental system to change this time. The Frisbee, the hand that propels it, and the air can be changed. Let us start by changing the size of the Frisbee.

After you have changed the size, you can change the material of the Frisbee. Repeat your experiments with foam plates, aluminum plates, and large plastic covers. Cardboard disks and metal paint can lids will also yield new data.

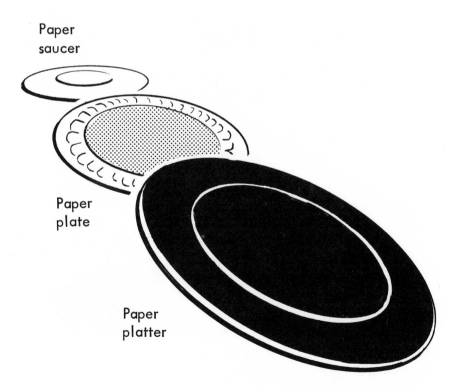

Paper
saucer

Paper
plate

Paper
platter

CHANGE THE SHAPE

Does a Frisbee have to be round and shaped like a plate? Would other shapes fly as well? Get out your scissors and start cutting to find out.

Square

Triangle

Free form

CHANGE THE SHAPE

Try putting some helicopter blades on your Frisbee.
How many blades would work best? Should these blades
be placed on top of or inside the Frisbee? Also try cutting
slots and holes in the disk, and you might add fins.

Helicopter blades above

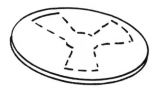

Helicopter blades inside

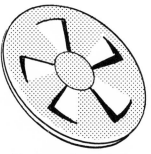

Slots used as blades

CHANGE THE SHAPE

The Australian boomerang was sailing long before the Frisbee. Experimenting with the boomerang will teach you much about your Frisbee because they are related in many ways.

Learn to ask specific questions of nature rather than the often used "How" or "Why" questions. Ask the boomerang, "If I doubled your weight, would you fly differently?" It will show you. Ask, "If I made you with three blades instead of two, would you fly farther?" It will show you. And you might ask, "If I slanted your blades, would you fly higher?" And again, the boomerang will present the data to you. These are called "If-and-would" data seeking questions.

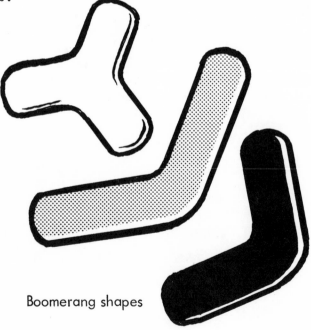

Boomerang shapes

CHANGE THE SHAPE

The Greeks invented the discus which is still another kind of Frisbee. A discus is thick in the middle, thin at the edge, and much heavier than a present-day Frisbee.

Tape two Frisbees together so that they take the shape of a discus. "What will be the difference in the flight of this new Frisbee?" you could ask first. Your Frisbee will tell you because you have asked it a specific question.

When you think that you are beginning to understand the differences which the new conditions are causing, you can change to "If-and-then" predictions to test your new knowledge.

Perhaps you think that because your Frisbee is now twice as heavy, it will sail twice as far. Make a prediction to test this idea. You can say to yourself, "If I double the weight of my Frisbee by taping two together like a discus, then I predict that it will go twice as far."

Always make your prediction before the experiment is started. A prediction is the best test of knowledge. If you can predict and usually be right, people will soon be following you around for your knowledge.

The discus-shaped Frisbee

Balance and
spin the Frisbee
on a pencil point.
Indent the under
side of the Frisbee
if the pencil slips.
Turn the Frisbee
over and try again.
Try this with foam
plates, metal
paint can lids,
and pie tins.

Spin a Frisbee
on a long bamboo
pole like a juggler.

Press gently on a
spinning Frisbee with
your finger. You
will sense some new data.

CHANGE THE WEIGHT

Multiply the object

Compare light and heavy Frisbees. Many times an object can be multiplied to change its weight. A foam plate can be a very light Frisbee. Hot candle wax can be dripped onto a paper plate to make a very heavy Frisbee. Also, try coating a paper plate with several layers of quick-dry paint.

It is important to change the distribution of the weight. Should the weight be concentrated at the center, at the rim, or distributed evenly? Heavy, round objects are easy to fasten to the center. It is harder to add weight evenly to the rim. Wire can be taped to the outside rim, or try taping coins or washers around the edge. Try the extra weight on the top and bottom sides of the plate. Which makes the most difference, the amount of weight or the position of the weight?

Here?...

Or here?

CHANGE THE SPIN

Tether the Frisbee so that you can watch it spin at close range. Stick a pin through the Frisbee and bend the point into a hook to which you can tie the string. Spin the Frisbee by hand and spin it with an electric gun drill. Put an eye bolt or a bent nail in the gun drill to support the string.

Next, loosen the lower end of the string and tie it to the rim of the Frisbee. Let it hang freely on the string. Start the Frisbee spinning with the electric gun drill, and you will see some surprising data.

Try different angles of spin.

Spin your Frisbee and swing it like a pendulum.

CHANGE THE SPIN

The amazing
bicycle wheel

While you are holding a bicycle wheel,
have a friend spin it as fast as he can. Still
holding the spinning wheel, try to run around
a rectangular table, making very sharp
corners. You will be amazed at what happens.

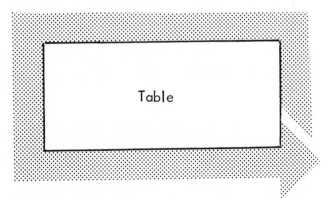

Table

SUGGESTED RULES FOR A TOURNAMENT

Keep score by counting the number of throws to hit
or to get into the target.

A Frisbee must have a paper plate base on which the
experimental changes are attached.

A Frisbee must land right side up to demonstrate its
gyroscopic character when thrown for distance. Throws
must be counted and repeated when the Frisbee turns
over like a plate.

A Frisbee must be within or beyond a line to be scored
at the highest value.

A Frisbee must be thrown cleanly through a hole target
to test for accuracy. A throw must be counted and
repeated if a branch or a sheet is hit or brushed.

A Frisbee must at least brush or knock bits of foliage
from a bush target.

At the free throw hole a score on the first throw is
a hole in one. A player who cannot put the Frisbee
down in five throws automatically gets a penalty score
of ten added points.

A Frisbee is disqualified when over half of it is damaged.

Low score wins.

SUGGESTED FRISBEE TARGETS

Disposal containers

Design your Frisbee course like a golf course to fit into and to take advantage of your own environment. Plastic waste baskets and disposal containers make excellent Frisbee "holes" or targets because they do little damage to the improvised disks. Brown bags, towels, and pillows also serve well as targets. Some of the holes or targets should be around or behind buildings or wide trees to test control of curved throws. One target should be a test for distance.

Sheets tied to poles are also soft targets. One sheet should test the boomerang property of gliding back to the thrower. The players throw to hit the back side of this sheet. Another sheet should have a hole in it through which the Frisbee must pass cleanly. This sheet is often used on the throw for distance.

The best hole is the free throw which is usually last. All contestants sit together in chairs around a large waste paper basket so that they can see at close range how the Frisbee of each opponent performs.

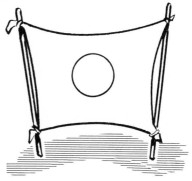

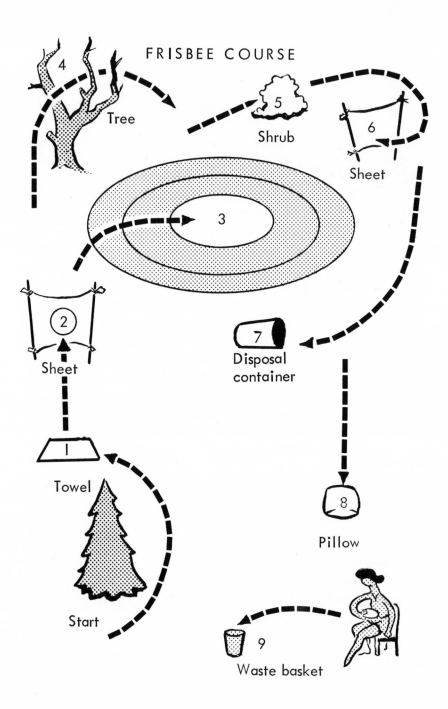

FRISBEE COURSE

4 Tree

5 Shrub

6 Sheet

3

2 Sheet

7 Disposal container

1 Towel

Start

8 Pillow

9 Waste basket

ORGANIZE A FRISBEE TEAM

After your tournament is completed, you can organize a Frisbee team. Send a challenge to other teams. You could play neighborhood, club, class, or school teams. One of the nice things about Frisbee as a sport is that anyone can learn to play it well if body contact is avoided. The following rules are suggested for team competition.

1. The playing field should be a rectangular athletic field.

2. The game should be thirty minutes long with fifteen minute halves.

3. Toss a coin to decide which team will throw off. The other team should decide the direction of its attack.

4. A goal is scored when an offensive player has two feet in the end zone after receiving a pass from a teammate.

5. Each time a goal is scored the teams should switch the direction of their attack.

6. The Frisbee may be thrown in any manner, but it must never be handed from player to player.

7. No player may walk, run, or take steps while holding the Frisbee.

8. Whenever the Frisbee is dropped, the other team may put it in play at that spot.

FRISBEE BIBLIOGRAPHY

The Frisbee is such a new invention that no books have been written about it yet. However, you are lucky because there is one good book about a related subject which is fun to read. Donald H. Menzel and Lyle G. Boyd have written The World of Flying Saucers. Frisbees and flying saucers have much in common. Also, look up the gyroscope in the encyclopedias and in other books to learn more about spinning motion.

Compton's Encyclopedia, 1974, Volume 26, pages 269-270

Merit Students' Encyclopedia, 1976, Volume 8, pages 343-344

World Book Encyclopedia, 1976, Volume 8, pages 436-438

THE CHALLENGE

Milk carton
package

From how high can you drop a fresh egg without breaking it? It is fun to watch an egg hit and splatter, but it is even more fun to see an egg drop a great distance and land unbroken.

Package engineering has become a fine art and an exciting profession. You will need this skill to get delicate Christmas presents through the mail unbroken. For the rest of your life you will be using many of the skills which you can develop while working on this problem.

It has been found that it is most convenient to pack the eggs in paper milk cartons so that every experimenter is working with the same conditions of difficulty. One-quart cartons present a challenge to experienced experimenters. Two-quart cartons are better for those who need more room in which to work.

Paper milk cartons have a roof-like top which can be opened and resealed easily. This gabled top is well adapted for attaching an identifying streamer. When the drop has been completed, the carton can be cut open quickly for examination with any sharp instrument.

Will it survive?

IT CAN BE DONE

The author started encouraging his students
to learn the art of packaging when NASA's Jet
Propulsion Laboratory in Pasadena was practicing
to land delicate instruments on the moon.

Early morning sunshine highlighted a helicopter two-thousand feet above Pasadena's
Rose Bowl. The pilot dropped four packaged eggs
into the predawn darkness below. Students
measured angles and ticked off seconds with
stopwatches as the eggs streaked silently down
to meet their fates. Scientists from the Jet
Propulsion Laboratory were surprised to hear
that three out of the four eggs had landed
unbroken.

Each year more skills are added to those
of experimenters from the years before. Most
of our experimenters meet their downfall from
the top of the California Institute of Technology's
new ten-story library building.

Eleven students have brought eggs down
unbroken from a mile-high plane. Three students
have been successful from two miles. What is
the limit? We are negotiating now to get our
eggs sent aloft in a rocket.

HOW STRONG IS AN EGG?

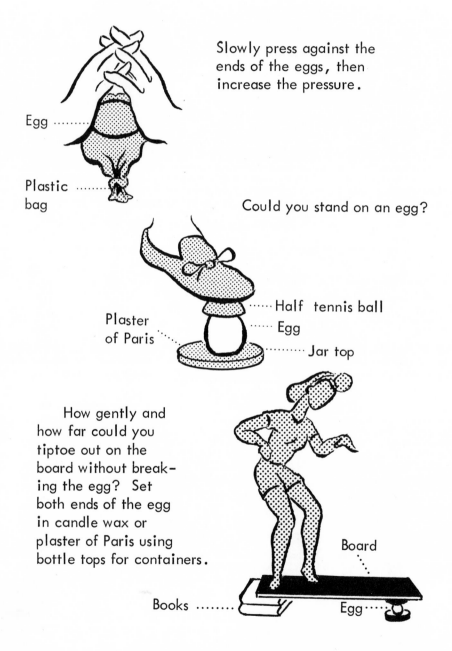

Slowly press against the
ends of the eggs, then
increase the pressure.

Egg

Plastic
bag

Could you stand on an egg?

Half tennis ball

Plaster
of Paris

Egg

Jar top

How gently and
how far could you
tiptoe out on the
board without break-
ing the egg? Set
both ends of the egg
in candle wax or
plaster of Paris using
bottle tops for containers.

Board

Books

Egg

DO NOT WASTE GOOD EGGS

There is no need to waste fresh eggs
in practice. Just ask your mother if you
can have more scrambled eggs and even
a few cheese omelets for the next few days.

Make it easier for her by
piercing the eggshells at both ends
with a darning needle or an ice pick.
Blow the contents of the egg into a
bowl and put the bowl in the refrig-
erator. Enlarging the bottom hole
can make the blowing easier.

Dry the eggshell and drip hot
candle wax on one hole. Then run
a small stream of water into the egg.
A gurgling sound will tell you how fast
the egg is filling. Seal the other hole
with hot candle wax.

The water-filled eggs are almost identical
in weight to fresh eggs. They barely sink
in fresh water. They will tell you much
about your packaging when you start experimenting. Don't forget that you can practice
with hard-boiled eggs also. And you can
eat them, too, after practice.

CONSIDER THIS

If you placed a small, plastic bag of water in a milk carton filled with water and dropped it out of a second story window, where would the bag of water go when the carton crashes onto the cement?

Ball   Block   Egg

If you dropped a foam cup of water with a Ping-Pong ball floating in it, what would happen to the ball? What would happen to a block of wood? To an egg floating in salt water?

Gravity will pull your egg down faster, faster, and faster until it reaches a steady speed because of friction with the air. This speed is called terminal velocity, and it is a little over one hundred miles per hour for the egg package. Finally the bottom of the carton touches the cement.

Quite suddenly now, in the egg's last few inches of descent, you must slow its speed down to zero miles per hour. This is quite a challenge; but others have done it, and you can do it.

In some way you must change all of the kinetic energy of the fall into heat, light, sound, electricity, friction, or mechanical energy.

The law of conservation of energy states that energy can never be lost. It can only be transformed into some other form of energy.

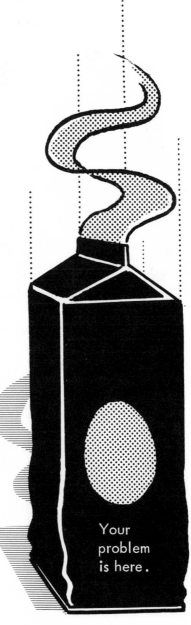

Your problem is here.

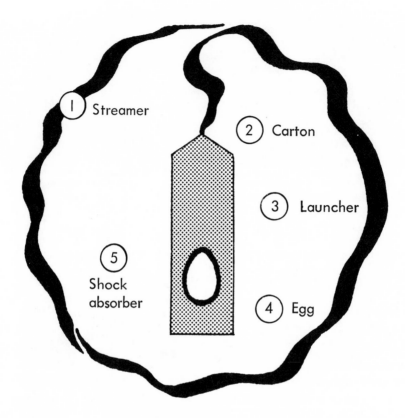

Experimenting is changing something purposely to learn more about it. "But how can you change an egg without breaking it?" you ask immediately. An easy way to see the possibilities for experimenting is to draw a sketch of all the objects and materials in the experimental system. Then draw a circle around them.

WHAT YOU CAN CHANGE

Now, concentrate on just these objects and materials. Make a list as shown below stating all the different ways which each can be changed. What new changes can you add to this list?

Change the carton
> Size, shape, weight, surface, attitude.
> Add nose cones, bumpers, and cushions.
> Substitute other cartons and containers.

Change the egg
> Size, shape, weight, position.
> Substitute a golf ball, Ping-Pong ball, and water.

Change the shock absorber
> Size, shape, weight, material.
> Try elasticity, crushability, padding, and cradling.

Change the streamer
> Size, shape, weight, material.
> Try flexibility and resistance.
> Change to fins and flaps for guidance.

Change the launcher
> Catapult, kite, helium balloon, skyscraper, helicopter, and airplane.

Why don't you start now making some changes in the carton to learn more about it? Let's just have some experimental fun gathering new data at first.

CHANGE THE CARTON

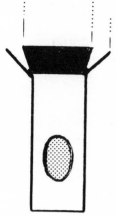

It is easy to fold back the gable sections and to use them as flaps. What can you invent to keep the flaps spread wide?

Should the egg be placed higher or lower in the carton?

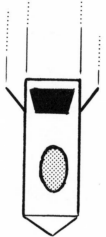

Cut flaps out of the sides of the carton and prop them out with toothpicks.

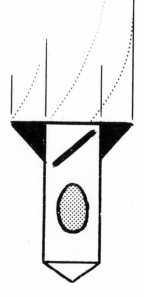

Cut triangular flaps from the sides and fold them out at an angle to make the carton spin as it descends.

CHANGE THE CARTON

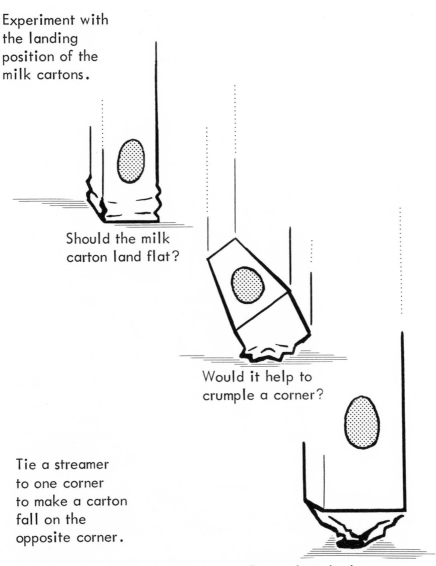

Experiment with
the landing
position of the
milk cartons.

Should the milk
carton land flat?

Would it help to
crumple a corner?

Tie a streamer
to one corner
to make a carton
fall on the
opposite corner.

Or would it be better
to crush a gable?

CHANGE THE SHOCK ABSORBER

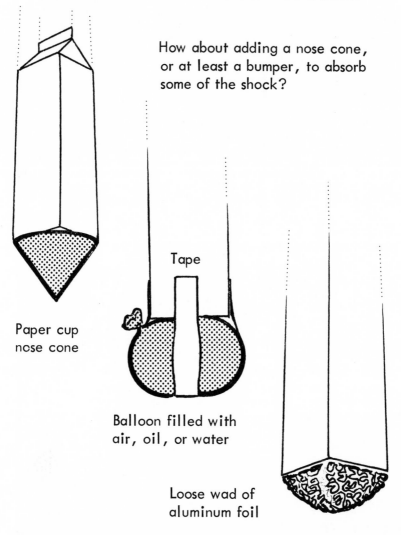

How about adding a nose cone, or at least a bumper, to absorb some of the shock?

Paper cup nose cone

Tape

Balloon filled with air, oil, or water

Loose wad of aluminum foil

Have you thought of changing the impact surface? You could move to grass or soft dirt. Try an impact onto a foam rubber pillow or mattress to protect the eggs.

CHANGE THE SHOCK ABSORBER

Try using the elasticity of rubber and of air for a shock absorber. A shock-absorbing filler for the carton could still be used with these elastic devices.

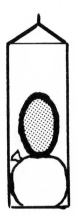

Put a small balloon of air under the egg.

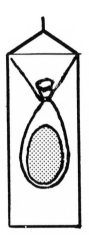

Hang the egg in a balloon on rubber bands.

Foam cups use friction as well as the elasticity of the air to absorb the shock of impact.

CHANGE THE SHOCK ABSORBER

Change the material which you will put inside the carton to insulate the egg from the shock of impact. Here are a few of the many possibilities:

Oil
Jello
Water
Bread
Cotton
Sawdust
Feathers
Balloons
Popcorn
Styrofoam
Urethane chips
Urethane foam
Paper shreds
Rubber bands
Puffed cereals

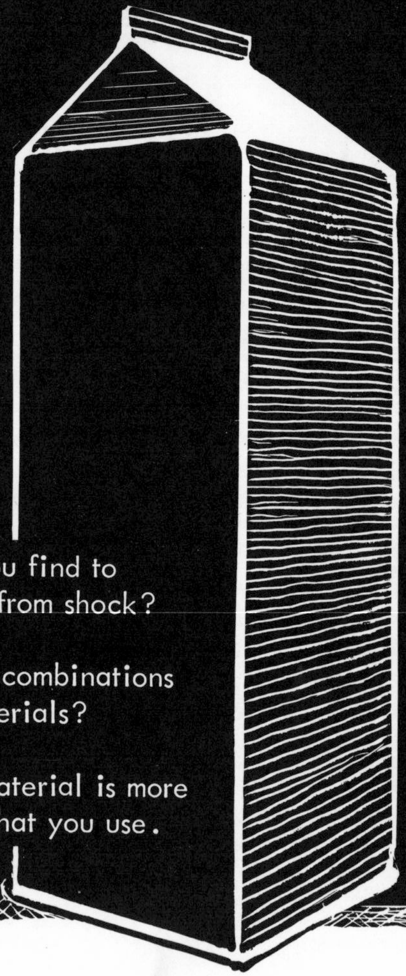

What else can you find to insulate the egg from shock?

How about using combinations of the above materials?

How you use a material is more important than what you use.

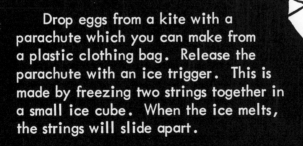

PREVENT THE SHOCK

Drop eggs from a kite with a parachute which you can make from a plastic clothing bag. Release the parachute with an ice trigger. This is made by freezing two strings together in a small ice cube. When the ice melts, the strings will slide apart.

Change the length,
shape, and weight
of the streamer.

Should the streamer
be single, double,
or multiple?

Would a looped
streamer as shown
to the left, bring
the egg down slower
than a straight
streamer?

Try paper, cloth,
and plastic ribbons
for streamers. Look
for new materials
with different
properties.

Would knots and
bows create more
resistance and slow
the carton?

Sew, staple, or glue
the streamer to the
milk carton.

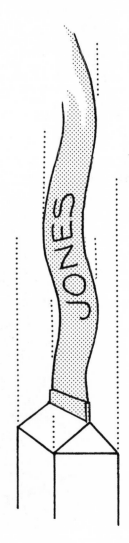

CHANGE THE STREAMER

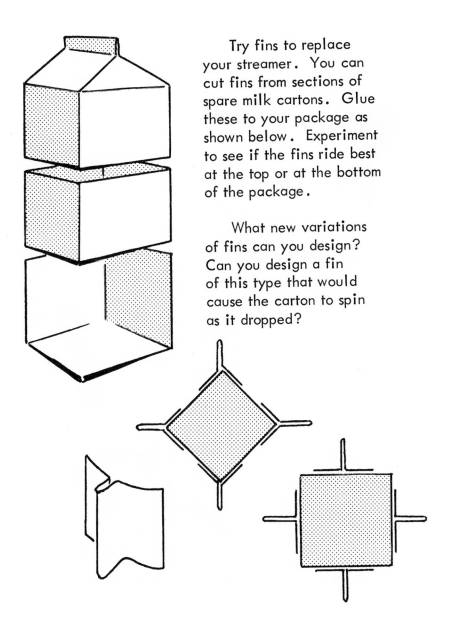

Try fins to replace your streamer. You can cut fins from sections of spare milk cartons. Glue these to your package as shown below. Experiment to see if the fins ride best at the top or at the bottom of the package.

What new variations of fins can you design? Can you design a fin of this type that would cause the carton to spin as it dropped?

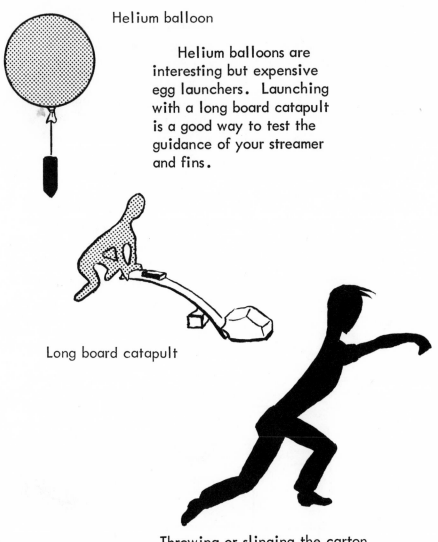

Helium balloon

Helium balloons are interesting but expensive egg launchers. Launching with a long board catapult is a good way to test the guidance of your streamer and fins.

Long board catapult

Throwing or slinging the carton is another good preliminary test.

CHANGE THE LAUNCH METHOD

Hand dropping out of building windows will be your most used test for packaged eggs. As you go higher, you must be sure that all of your experimenters and all of your spectators are clear of the target area. Getting hit on the head by an egg package from a skyscraper is like being hit by a batted baseball. It is suggested that safety helmets be worn.

SUGGESTED RULES FOR AN EGG DROP

These rules should be varied for the abilities of the participants and for the kinds of materials which are available. When you make your own rules, just be sure that everyone gets the same fair chance to be successful.

Use a fresh chicken egg unless some other kind is available to all participants.

Use one-quart, paper milk cartons for packages. Younger experimenters sometimes prefer two-quart cartons.

Any material may be used for shock insulation on low drops. Sand, water, and oil are eliminated when they might become a liability on high drops.

The egg should not be taped or cast in a solid. The carton must be opened easily to display the egg.

Use a streamer no longer than three meters. It should be no wider than the milk carton.

Identify the entry well with a wide felt pen. Print your name on the streamer, on the bottom, and on the four sides of the carton.

The use of fins, flaps, nose cones, and bumpers often gets discussed in rule making. This is especially true for high altitude drops because these items are hard to pack in a box for an air drop.

SELECT A GOOD DROP AREA

An egg drop will draw a crowd in a hurry. Invite your friends to the low drops. When you try for height, you must be careful because the spectators can become a problem and a liability. Even the participants themselves can get in the way of falling packages if they are not organized.

Therefore the drop area and the time of the drop must be given careful consideration. Plan preliminary drops at schools to avoid mob scenes. Be sure that you can control the spectators before you ask permission for a high drop from a public building. High drops are usually made at sunrise before many people appear on the streets going to work. Egg drops must be cancelled when the wind starts blowing toward the building.

When eggs are to be dropped from a helicopter or from an airplane, the landing area must be selected very carefully to protect curious bystanders who are always attracted. As you send eggs higher and higher, you must be prepared to spend more time finding them. At a mile high you will find it hard to see an egg carton in a glaring sky. Seek an amateur radio operator who could be interested in dropping a radio "beeper" with your eggs.

When you have chosen the drop site, a drop master should be designated. Everyone wants this job. But from high buildings it can only be an adult. The drop master should check to see that all cartons and streamers are colorfully decorated and identified. Spectators always want to know immediately whose eggs were most successfully packed.

71

PREPARE A TARGET

As you go higher, prepare a target for the eggs. Put a plastic sheet on the ground and put a round cardboard target in the middle of this protective covering.

Choose a target master who will be in charge of this drop area and of the cleanup crew. Eggs and their protective liquids and jells have been known to splash on walls, doors, and windows. Plastic sheets can be taped to walls for protection. The cleanup crew should be responsible for bringing a box with wash rags and drying towels as well as detergents and cleansing powders. This crew should see that a broom and a large cardboard box are ready for the disposal of the unsuccessful eggs. Sometimes the only cleanup needed is to fold up the plastic drop sheet and put it into the disposal container.

Another dependable person should be selected to open the cartons when they are dropped. A double door opening should be cut in one side of the carton. Successful eggs should be photographed in their cartons and saved for display.

Target master / Opener / Cleanup crew

The target area

BOX THE CARTONS FOR HIGH DROPS

All the cartons of finalists should be placed loosely in a small cardboard box with their streamers rolled and ready to be dropped. It is important that all the packages be dropped closely together to eliminate needless hours of searching. The cartons are then transported to the airport without being disturbed again and are placed aboard the aircraft. Upon being dropped, a student-made parachute can jerk the cartons out together.

The local parachute training center has been quite interested in our project, but we have been careful not to bring too many eggs to them at one time. We pay for our eggs to be lifted just as we would pay to be taken aloft for practice parachute jumps. The egg droppers share the expense of the drop.

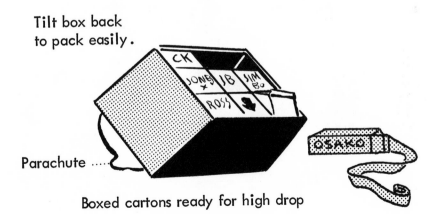

Tilt box back to pack easily.

Parachute ....

Boxed cartons ready for high drop

Move backward until you can sight the drop master at a forty-five degree angle with a sighting device. Now the distance to the target will equal the height of the drop. Having this data and the elapsed time of the drop in seconds, you can calculate the downward speed of your egg in miles per hour.

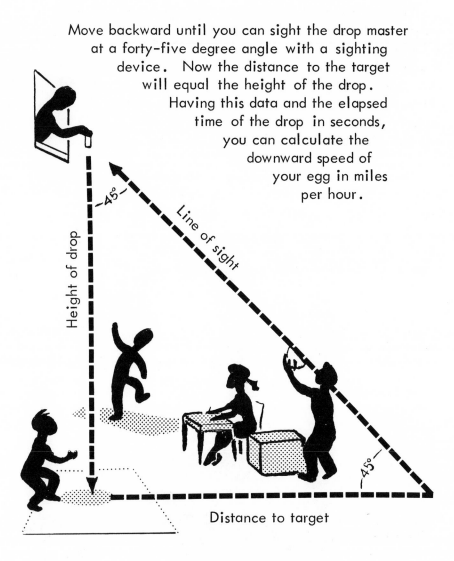

Height of drop

45°

Line of sight

45°

Distance to target

74

DISPLAY THE EGGS

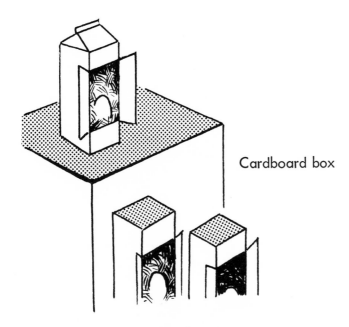

Cardboard box

Dropped cartons can be given
to an official opener who should cut
double doors on one side of each carton.
For display purposes, punch pencil holes
through the back sides of the milk cartons
and poke other holes in the sides of a
cardboard box. Hang the cartons from
these holes with S-hooks made from paper
clips. Spectators can view the results
then without handling. Eggs have been
known to drop a mile and survive only to
have someone drop them carelessly onto
a table to break.

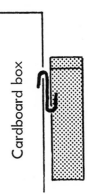

Cardboard box

EGG DROP BIBLIOGRAPHY

Ask your librarian to help you find the following books which will suggest still more experimental fun with eggs. Then read all that you can about the natural phenomena related to the egg drop in science books.

Milgrom	Egg-Ventures
Pflug	Egg-Speriments
Wyler and Robinson	Science Teasers, page 5

Compton's Encyclopedia, 1974

Galileo	Volume 11, page 5
Gravitation	Volume 11, pages 194-197
Shock absorber	Volume 17, page 21

Merit Students' Encyclopedia, 1976

Galileo	Volume 7, pages 441-444
Gravitation	Volume 8, pages 194-195
Momentum	Volume 12, page 400

World Book Encyclopedia, 1976

Arch	Volume 1, pages 555-557
Egg	Volume 6, page 78
Galileo	Volume 8, pages 11-12
Gravitation	Volume 8, pages 320-323
Momentum	Volume 13, pages 582-583
Packaging	Volume 15, page 16
Velocity	Volume 20, page 238

CHAPTER FIVE

TOOTHPICK BRIDGES

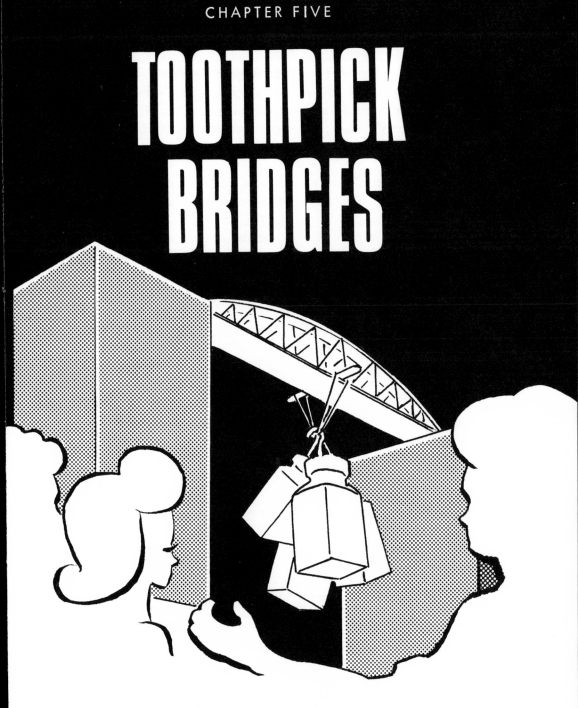

CAN YOU BUILD A TOOTHPICK BRIDGE
THAT WILL HOLD THE MOST WEIGHT?

THE PROBLEM

How strong can you build a toothpick bridge? Can you build a bridge on which you can stand? Can you build a bridge that will hold weights like the one on the title page for this chapter? Using the same number of toothpicks, can you build a better bridge than your friends or classmates?

The best test of the strength of a model bridge is to hang weights from it. First put a pencil or a flat stick across the middle. Then loop a circle of string to make a bridle over the ends of the stick. Now it will be easy to add weights until the model bridge cracks or tumbles into the "canyon."

In this way you can tell where your design is weak. The experimental fun begins with the rebuilding to make the bridge stronger. It will make you feel so much more comfortable when you cross a high bridge on your next vacation trip.

When your highway department needs a bridge for one of its new roads, it prints the specifications which tell exactly how it wants the bridge to be built. These are commonly called "specs." Engineers bid for the job. The engineer who can build the bridge with the least amount of materials and still pass the safety tests can earn a good living at this work. Anyone can build a very strong bridge with unlimited resources. But no one, including the taxpayers, can afford that kind of a bridge.

The following page of specs was given by the author to one of his science classes which wanted to build toothpick bridges. Why don't you read it and try to build your own bridge?

SPECS FOR A TOOTHPICK BRIDGE

Your bridge will
be tested like
this.

It must span a
canyon which
is 15 cm. wide.

Use only standard, flat, wooden toothpicks.

The size limits are: Length 20 cm., width 6 cm.,
and height 10 cm. A toothpick is 6 cm. long.

You may use up to fifty toothpicks or parts, and
you may use four long matchstick girders.

Use only quick-dry model glue. The wood of
the toothpicks is to remain natural except at the
glued ends. Do not spray them.

The roadbed should have a clearance of 5 cm.
wide by 5 cm. high. Cut a paper roadbed of
typing paper, identify it with your last name,
and glue it on the floor of your bridge.

25 grams

One of the most popular fishing weights is cast approximately to the size and shape shown here. These weights can be made into very accurate measuring weights by filing and sanding them.

50 grams

Another good kind of weight for your experimenting is made from the plastic medicine bottles which are discarded each day at the pharmacies. They can be filled very accurately when sand is used for the weight. String loops can be tied quickly to the necks of the bottles. Visit a science class and ask permission to use an accurate scale.

100 grams

Once you have one set of good weights, you can duplicate them easily at home with a simple balance beam. Be sure to include the cap and the string for the loop in the total weight.

In addition to the weights shown here, you should have plastic bottle weights of 200 grams, 500 grams, and 1,000 grams. The 1,000 gram weight is called a kilogram.

MAKE YOUR OWN WEIGHTS

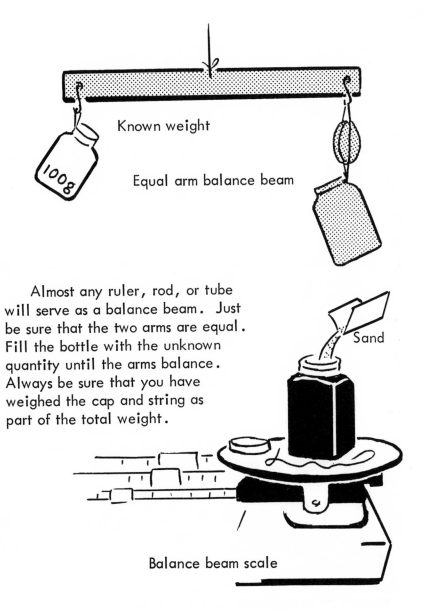

Known weight

Equal arm balance beam

Almost any ruler, rod, or tube will serve as a balance beam. Just be sure that the two arms are equal. Fill the bottle with the unknown quantity until the arms balance. Always be sure that you have weighed the cap and string as part of the total weight.

Sand

Balance beam scale

Draw a 15 cm. canyon like this on a sheet of typing paper. The canyon should be about as wide as a page of this book. Then design a bridge to span your canyon drawing.

The bridge illustrated on the title page of this chapter was not suggested as a best design. It is just one possibility for solving the problem of crossing this canyon.

With a single line draw a roadbed across the chasm. Then think about how to support the roadbed. Sketch a single 6 cm. line for each toothpick which you will use. Where will each toothpick do the most good?

Once you start thinking about this, you may want to make several sketches to consider the different ways to support this bridge. But which shape is best? How could you find out? You could find a book about building bridges in the library; you could talk with a bridge engineer; but you could have much more fun inquiring of your models. Just ask them, and they will tell you which is best.

BUILD YOUR BRIDGE

Build your bridge right on your drawing. Place all the toothpicks for one whole side together on the sketch. You may want to cut some toothpicks shorter with a razor blade. Put a drop of quick-dry model glue on the end of each toothpick. In a few minutes that whole side of the bridge can be pulled carefully from the paper sketch before the glue is dry. Then the other side can be set up in the same way. Finally the two sides can be held up with clothes pins and joined by additional toothpicks. Large paper clips and hair clips are also used as holders during the drying process. Let the glue dry over night before testing is begun. Glue a paper roadbed into your bridge after printing your last name on it with a felt pen.

Paper clips   Quick-dry glue

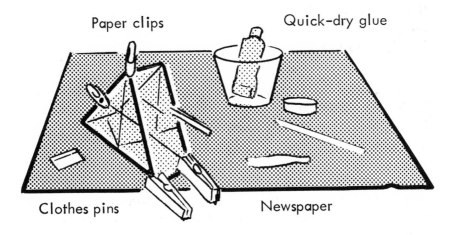

Clothes pins   Newspaper

Dry the glue over night.

CHANGE SOMETHING TO LEARN MORE

After you have built a bridge, you may be wondering if it is the very best bridge that you can build. You can find out for yourself by experimenting.

Remember that experimenting is making purposeful changes to learn more about something. Usually you can change a condition. A condition is a state of being. When you change a condition and get a different result, you must decide which is better. By putting all the best conditions and all the best materials together you finally will be able to build a super bridge.

Always keep everything the same for each experiment except that you will change one condition which is called the "variable." Then you will be able to tell if this condition does make a difference and whether it is better. This is called "keeping control" of an experiment.

Inquire of nature when you have a problem. Nature is by far your best authority. Nature can tell you more than books, more than teachers, and more than scientists. This is where scientists get all their knowledge. They tell us that they have merely scratched the surface of knowledge to be learned from nature. When you want to know something special about your bridges, be sure to ask your bridges. Ask them specific questions, and they will give you answers.

Following are some bridge problems which you should investigate. These problems involve different conditions.

CHANGE THE POSITION OF THE TOOTHPICK

Can a toothpick hold more weight on its end or on its side? Devise some kind of experimental test that gives both positions the same fair chance to hold up the weights.

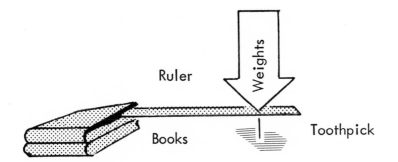

Add weights over the end of the toothpick until it breaks. Steady the ruler with the book cover.

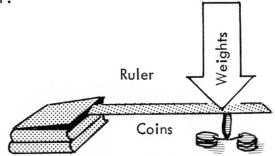

Transfer the force of the weights from the ruler through a coin on edge to the toothpick lying bridged on its side across two stacks of coins.

TRIANGULAR VERSUS PLANK

One of the first decisions many young bridge builders must make is whether to build a flat, compact, plank bridge or to build an open, airy bridge. Does solidness always produce strength? Use the same number of toothpicks for each bridge and glue only the ends of the toothpicks.

Consider the forces involved in your experimenting. Gravity is the main force that will be straining your bridge. It will be trying to collapse it and to attract it toward the center of the earth. When automobiles cross a bridge, even with a heavy load, gravity does not increase suddenly. Instead, it will be trying to drag that extra weight through the bridge to the bottom of the canyon. What shape is best for a bridge which must hold up under extreme loading?

Which bridge is stronger?

Plank bridge

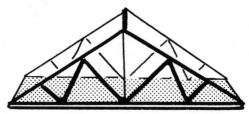

Open triangular bridge

Will a triangle made with three toothpicks hold up as much weight as a square which is made of four toothpicks?

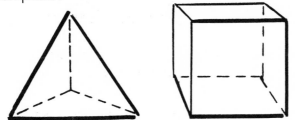

Will a pyramid made with six toothpicks hold up as much weight as a cube made of ten toothpicks?

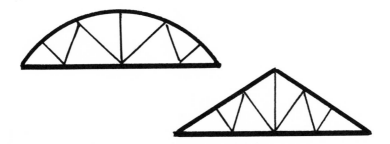

Roman arches are known for their strength.
Compare an arch design with a triangular design.

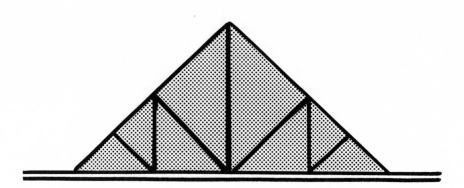

Another possibility that you should investigate is:
Should the bridge be supported from above or from below?

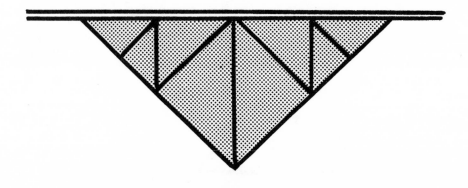

Think about the strain on each long beam. Would it be
the same for each of the above positions? Would a bridge
be twice as strong if you supported it both from above and
from below? Try and see.

CHANGE TO ANOTHER KIND OF BRIDGE

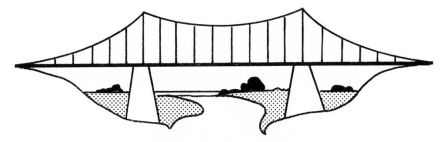

Suspension bridge made with thread and cardboard

Soda
straw
bridge

Make a soda straw bridge by putting the parts in place and wiping the ends with a hot nail or needle. A soldering iron with a temperature control makes a fine tool for welding plastic straws. Soda straw and suspension bridges tend to become much larger than the toothpick bridges.

Try a keystone bridge made with urethane foam blocks cut with a razor blade.

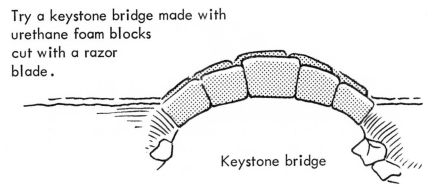

Keystone bridge

SUGGESTED WAYS TO TEST BRIDGES

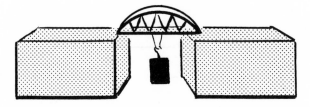

Make a 15 cm. canyon between two boxes
or push two tables that distance apart.

Make a wood test stand with a 15 cm. canyon
between the upright boards.

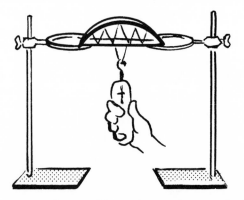

Borrow two ringstands and a spring scale from the
science teacher at your school. Pull on the scale
until the bridge cracks or fails.

WHOSE BRIDGE IS BEST?

Young bridge builders usually want their models tested with hanging weights. Testing with spring scales is faster, but this method is not as accurate. It is very exciting and informing to watch these bridges being tested.

Advanced experimenters sometimes use a formula which gives more credit to the builders who pass the specs with the use of a minimum of material. One such formula is to divide the weight of the bridge into the load that it holds. If Susan can build a bridge that is as strong as John's bridge and if she can do it using only half the material, she must be a far better bridge builder.

Susan's bridge   John's bridge

Holds   2000 grams   Holds   2000 grams
Weighs   5 grams   Weighs   10 grams

$$5\overline{)2000}\ \ 400\text{ points}$$ $$10\overline{)2000}\ \ 200\text{ points}$$

Some experimenters divide once again by the number of toothpicks which the builder has used. This gives even more credit to those who use each toothpick to the greatest advantage. If Susan had used sixty toothpicks and if John had used ninety-six, their scores would then look like this:

$$60\overline{)400}\ \ 66.6\text{ points}$$ $$96\overline{)200}\ \ 2.08\text{ points}$$

BRIDGE BIBLIOGRAPHY

When you finish experimenting with your bridges, you will appreciate reading about other people's bridges. Look up key words such as gravity, beam, tension, compression, cohesion, suspension, and abutment.

Britannica Junior Encyclopedia, 1975, Volume 3, pages 339–348

Compton's Encyclopedia, 1974, Volume 2, pages 321–328

Merit Students' Encyclopedia, 1976, Volume 2, pages 419–424

World Book Encyclopedia, Volume 2, pages 490–495

Billings	Bridges
Bryant	Children's Book of Celebrated Bridges
Chester	The Builder of the Golden Gate Bridge
Doherty	Bridges
Goldwater	Bridges and How They Are Built
Gramet	Highways Across Waterways
Holland	Big Bridge
Peet	First Book of Bridges
Saunders	Building the Brooklyn Bridge
Steinman	Famous Bridges of the World

CHAPTER SIX

WINDMILLS

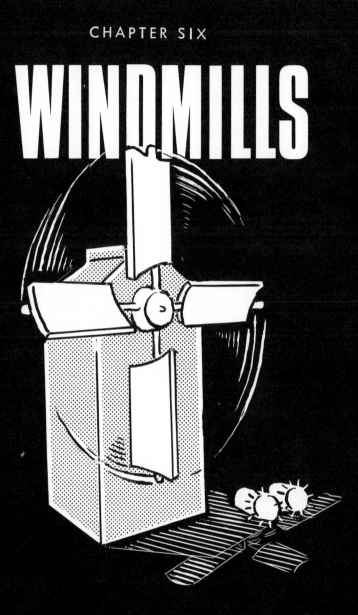

CAN YOU BUILD A WINDMILL THAT
WILL LIFT THE GREATEST WEIGHT?

THE PROBLEM

Can you build a windmill that will lift a weight more quickly than a friend's windmill? Would your windmill lift a heavier weight? How many kinds of work can you make your windmill do? You can choose any of these problems for your experimenting. Then compare your windmill with those of your friends.

The windmill was one of the first machines to make use of free energy provided by nature. Windmills have ground grain, pumped water, sawed wood, and pounded ore through much of history. Motors have been replacing them, but they are being built again because we must conserve our fossil fuels.

Experimenting is changing something to learn more about it. However, be sure that you are changing only one condition at a time. You must keep control of your experimenting. If you change several variables in an experiment and if you notice a spectacular difference in the result, what caused it? You don't know. There is no way that you can tell which of the several changed conditions caused it. You must start all over again changing just one condition at a time until you find the one which caused the spectacular change. Be sure that you start with all conditions under control except your experimental variable. Have fun now building your windmill and making the changes which will help it to work better.

Two-quart, paper milk
cartons make fine windmills.
The polyethylene plastic
bottles serve well, too,
but they are much harder
to cut. Cut out the bot-
tom if you plan to lift
weights with a pulley.
If you are not going to
do this, add a heavy
piece of wood or metal
to the bottom for stability
when you are using a
strong wind.

Milk carton
mill building

Paper
cone
roof

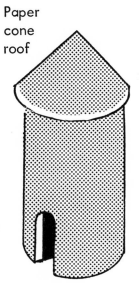

Cardboard tube
mill building

CHANGE THE SHAPE OF THE BLADE

Curved sections
from foam cups

Change the number
of blades.

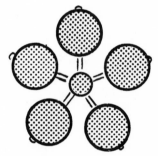

Round, flat
foam saucers

And change the
material of the blades:

Notecards
Cardboard
Balsa wood
Foam cups
Foam sheets
Cloth

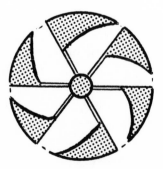

Triangular sails

CHANGE THE SPOKES OF THE FAN

What would be the best number
of spokes? Should there be two,
four, six, or more?

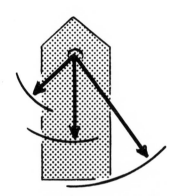

Should the spokes be long or short?
It is best that they do not hit your
table, but they could pass beyond
the edge.

Spokes can be part
of an aluminum or
of a paper plate.
Bend the vanes
to the desired pitch.

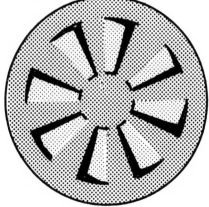

CHANGE THE HUB

The hub can be two
shortened foam cups
taped together. It is
easy to thrust spokes
through the foam.
Corks are often used.
Spools serve well if
you can drill holes in
the wood.

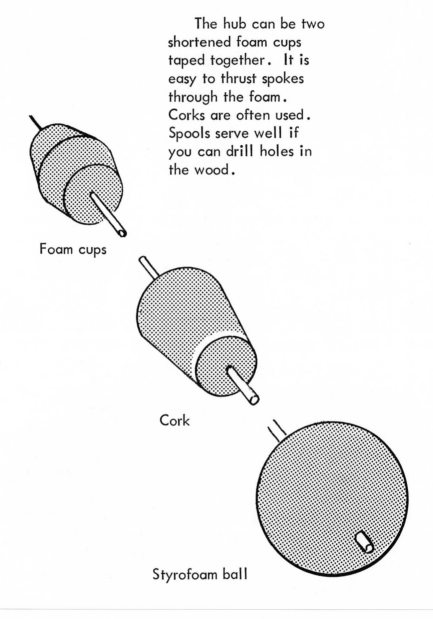

Foam cups

Cork

Styrofoam ball

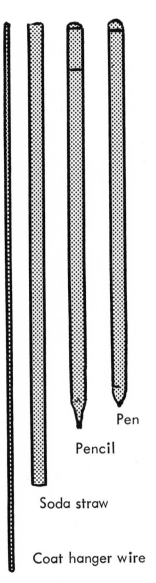

Pencil

Pen

Soda straw

Coat hanger wire

Pencils just happen
to fit holes in spools.

A coat hanger axle can
be bent with a U-shape
to give it crankshaft action.

Use a tape bushing
to make a tight fit
between the axle and
the hub of the fan.

CHANGE THE PULLEY

Do you want power,
or do you want speed?
You can have both, but
you cannot have them at
the same time. Try dif-
ferent sizes of pulleys
until you get the result
for which you are looking.

The axle
is a pulley.

A spool
is a pulley.

Pulley size is measured
in the groove of the wheel
rather than at the outside
diameter. Tape is a good
bushing to make spools
and reels fit snugly to
small axles like coat hanger
wires.

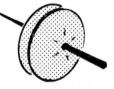

A movie reel
is a large pulley.

You can quickly make
any size pulley that you
want by wrapping masking
tape around the axle.
Glue notecard or card-
board disks to the sides
of the tape for flanges
to keep the pulley belt
in place.

Masking tape
can make any
size of pulley.

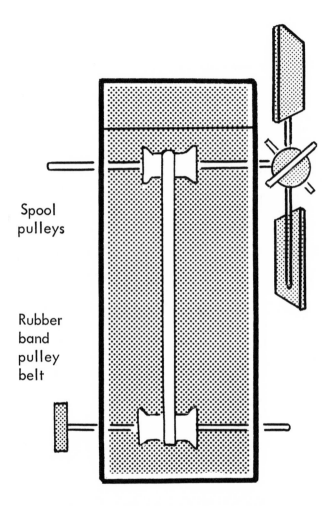

Spool
pulleys

Rubber
band
pulley
belt

This setup was used for power in early colonial sawmills. Water pumps, grindstones, and lathes could be added to the axle at the bottom of the mill building. If you must use a string for a pulley belt, coat the pulley with rubber cement to prevent slipping.

CHANGE PULLEYS TO GEARS

Gears are pulleys with teeth. They cannot slip. You can make your gears from foam, cork, and wood with pins or small nails for teeth. Be sure to clip the heads off the pins or nails. Gears can transfer energy in a different direction so that you can put simple machines on a horizontal axle. See what differences you can make now in speed and power by changing the size of each gear.

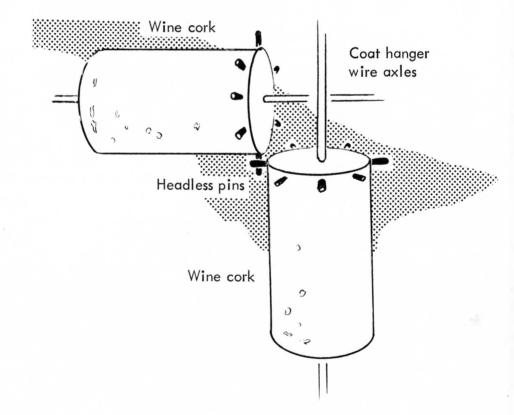

Wine cork

Coat hanger wire axles

Headless pins

Wine cork

CHANGE THE WIND

Your experimental wind will usually be from a ventilation fan because it is so easy to control. Your windmill can be placed at any distance. Make a wind tunnel for even better control. Just wrap a plastic sheet around a fan and some ice cream cartons and tape them together.

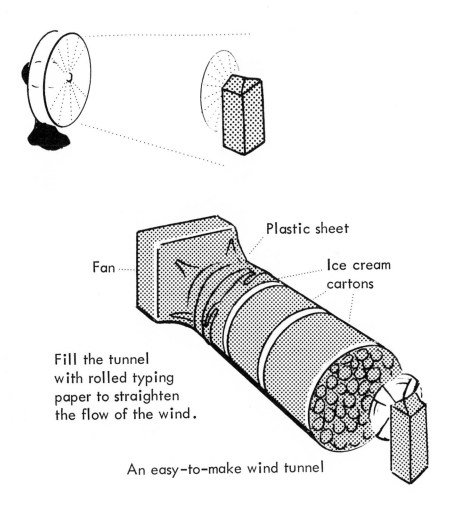

Plastic sheet

Fan

Ice cream cartons

Fill the tunnel with rolled typing paper to straighten the flow of the wind.

An easy-to-make wind tunnel

WINDMILL BIBLIOGRAPHY

You can find many paintings and drawings of windmills in the library, but there are only a few books which will help you. In the reference books key words to look for are windmills, levers, pulleys, and gears.

Beedell   Windmills

Brangwyn   Windmills

Hopkins   Old Watermills and Windmills

Reynolds   Windmills and Watermills

Spier   Of Dikes and Windmills

Britannica Junior Encyclopedia, 1975, Volume 15, page 124

Compton's Encyclopedia, 1974, Volume 26, page 177

World Book Encyclopedia, 1976, Volume 21, page 281

CHAPTER SEVEN

FIRE BOWS

CAN YOU START A FIRE FASTEST
WITH AN INDIAN FIRE BOW?

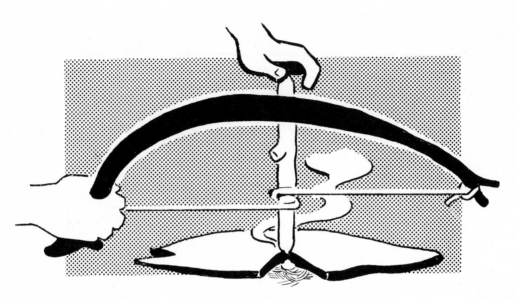

Can you make smoke faster than your friends with an Indian fire bow? Could you start a fire with one if your life depended on it in an emergency? You will have a fine feeling of security when you know how to do this. You will be very proud of yourself when you learn this very important survival skill.

Making fire with the fire bow is by far the hardest problem presented in this book. If you can make smoke, you are close to making fire. However, this last stage of the process is hard to regulate because you cannot see the gases. You must blow away the suffocating smoke and replace it with fresh oxygen. You will learn to do this only with practice. Don't give up easily when you find yourself close to success. You can experiment best with a partner on this problem.

HAVE A PURPOSE IN MIND

This last chapter has a slightly different format to help you improve the design of your experiments now that you have had considerable practice. The wording of each suggested experiment has been left unfinished so that you can think more about the purpose which you have in mind before you start each experiment.

If you need information because you do not have any data to think about, you can ask an "If-would" question. The suggested experiment might be, "If I try a straight stick for a bow instead of a curved branch, (pause and think) what would happen?" You really don't know, and you want to find out. If-would questions lead you into data-seeking experiments.

When you are beginning to understand the fire bow, you should begin designing a different kind of experiment. Change the conditions again and go to extremes to test your understanding. Make "If-then" statements with predictions. Your fire bow will tell you how right or how wrong you are. You should design the same experiment this way now: "If I try a straight stick for a bow instead of a curved branch, (pause and think) then I predict that the cord will rub too much." Your fire bow will tell you how good your prediction is. This was a prediction statement with the purpose of testing understanding.

Remember now, if you need data, ask an "If-would" question. If you want to test your knowledge of the fire bow, make an "If-then" statement with a prediction.

MATERIALS WHICH YOU WILL NEED

Fire bow — Use inflexible, straight and curved sticks and branches. Try dowels and bamboo.

Cord — Use any strong, rough cord. Boot laces and leather thongs are often used.

Bearing — This will protect your hand as you hold the fire stick. Make it from a block of wood, rock, shell, or any insulator with a small depression in it.

Fire stick — This spinning stick is usually a hard wood. Cut a straight branch. Dowels work well.

Base — Softer woods are used for the baseboard. Cut a notch to the side of the drill hole for fresh air and oxygen. This notch also collects the hot, charred sawdust.

Tinder — Tinder is any easy-to-start-on-fire material. Pioneers used charred cloth. Indians favored dry grasses and plant fibers. A good practice tinder which is easy to get is lens paper such as is used to clean eyeglasses and microscope lenses.

THE FIRE TRIANGLE THEORY

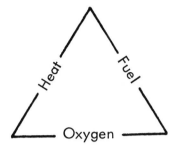

There will come a time when you will be making smoke, and you will probably be tired by that time. You may even feel like giving up. This is when you must try harder because you are so close to making fire. The fire triangle theory may help you at this critical point. This theory says that you must have three ingredients to start a fire: fuel, heat, and oxygen.

Your fuel will be the hot sawdust which will be rubbed loose from the fire stick and the base. The wood will begin to break down fast as it begins to char. Then you will add more fuel in the form of tinder, which is used because it flashes into fire quickly once you produce the first spark.

Heat will be supplied by the frictional rubbing of the fire stick on the baseboard. The heat will accumulate. Try not to stop spinning the fire stick and let it cool.

Oxygen is by far the most difficult ingredient with which you must work. When you begin making smoke, focus your attention at the bottom of the fire stick. You must try to blow away the smothering smoke fumes and replace them with fresh air which supplies the oxygen. You must develop techniques for doing this without losing your heat.

CHANGE THE BOW

Wood coat hanger bow

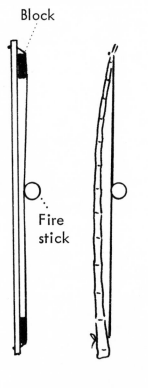

Meter stick

Bamboo stick

Pause and think for a moment of your purpose when you come to the comma in these suggested experiments.

If I try a straight piece of wood like a meter stick instead of a bow, ...

If I use a shorter (and a longer) bow, ...

If I use a bamboo bow, ...

If I use a metal bow, ...

If I use a curved-wood saw handle for a bow, ...

If I try an archer's bow, ...

If I use the bow as a rocker instead of as a push-pull device, ...

Now, what new experiments can you design by changing the bow?

CHANGE THE CORD

Try having a friend help you with the bow.
Try hand loops on the cord instead of the bow.

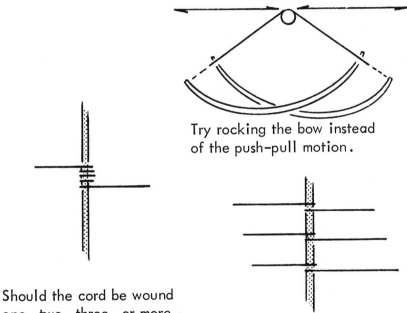

Try rocking the bow instead
of the push-pull motion.

Should the cord be wound
one, two, three, or more
times around the fire stick?

How many helpers can
you use on one fire stick?

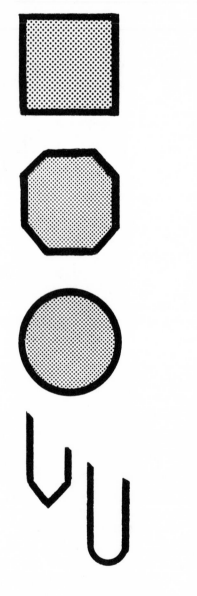

If I practice spinning the stick with an electric gun drill so that I can blow the smoke more easily, ...

If I use a square (and an octagonal) stick instead of a round one, ...

If I use a narrower (and a wider) fire stick, ...

If I make the fire stick of soft wood instead of hard wood, ...

If I roughen the smooth, burned and blackened point with sand-paper, ...

If I use a shorter (and a longer) fire stick, ...

If I make the bottom end more pointed (and more blunt), ...

If I spin the fire stick slower (and faster), ...

If I saw a couple of cross grooves through the pointed end of the fire stick to admit more fresh air, ...

CHANGE THE BEARING

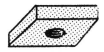

You must have a bearing to protect the hand that holds the top of the spinning fire stick. You can wear a glove, and you can lubricate the bearing with candle wax to reduce the heat.

Ancient fire makers used stones and shells with natural depressions. A block of wood with a slight depression carved with a knife is most commonly used now. The depression will wear fast into the desired shape to fit the pointed end of the fire stick.

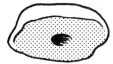

Manufactured, cup-shaped objects such as small, metal bottle caps and gas pipe caps will work well especially when insulated. Pound a nail into the end of the fire stick and hold it with any object which has a hole in it.

Try all of these. Then invent a few more of your own. Use the one that works best for you.

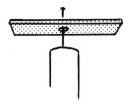

CHANGE THE BASEBOARD

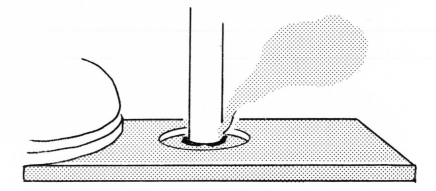

If I put sand in the drill hole to roughen the surfaces, ...

If I try softer (and harder) woods, ...

If I use thinner (and thicker) baseboards, ...

If I use the baseboard out in the warm sun instead of in the cool shade, ...

If I use other materials like cardboard for the baseboard in place of the wood, ...

If I tack the baseboard down to the floor so that it cannot wiggle, ...

CHANGE THE NOTCH IN THE BASE

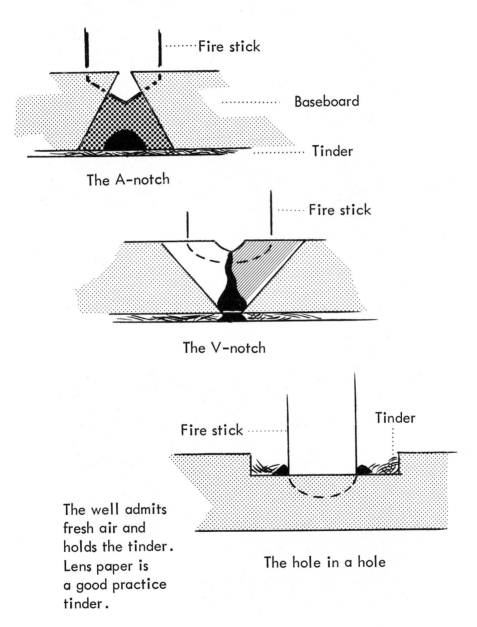

Fire stick

Baseboard

Tinder

The A-notch

Fire stick

The V-notch

Fire stick

Tinder

The well admits
fresh air and
holds the tinder.
Lens paper is
a good practice
tinder.

The hole in a hole

CHANGE TO A HAND DRILL

The hand drill was used as a fire making device by early people who lived in a very hot climate with special woods. You will find this very hard to do. But, try and see what happens.

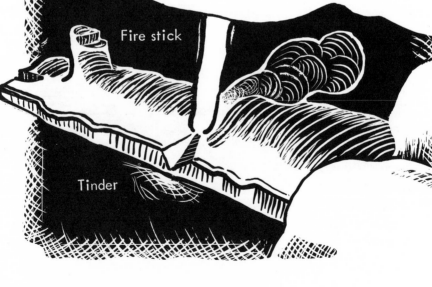

Fire stick

Tinder

116

CHANGE TO A FIRE DRILL
(First Cousin of the Fire Bow)

The fire drill was used with an arrowhead by the early Egyptians to hollow out stones which were to be used as vases. Sometimes these drills were quite large, and it took several men to turn the spindle. When the Assyrians started using iron, the fire drill with a nail at the end became the carpenter's drill.

Some of the ancient survival authorities preferred the fire drill to the fire bow because they could put gravity to work to help them. Almost any string can be used with the fire drill. The fire bow demands a strong cord. The string of the fire drill is usually passed through the hole at the top of the fire stick and tied to the two ends of a horizontal pump bar. A heavy weight, which does not have to be round, is tied and balanced to the fire stick.

Wind up the string with its pump bar. Then press downward to start the fire drill in motion. The momentum of the spinning weight will rewind the string for each pumping motion. You can repeat all of your fire bow experiments with the fire drill.

CHANGE THE PUMP

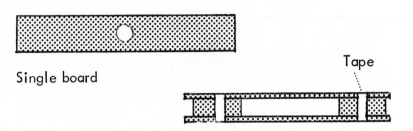

Single board

Tape

Two rulers

If I use a single stick with no hole and just pump up and down beside the spinning stick, ...

If I use two or three folds of cardboard in place of the wood baseboard, ...

If I use two rulers separated by two blocks and taped them together, ...

If I eliminate the pump board (as shown below) and tie two loops on a long cord so that my friend can pull back and forth with me, ...

Hand loops can eliminate the pump board.

CHANGE THE CORD

Try nylon fishing
line, string, twine,
cord, and rope for
the pump. Be sure
to change the way
that you attach the
cord to the spinning
fire stick.

Always try all
possible conditions,
and then pick the
best that will help
to solve your
problem.

Go to extremes
as you change the
conditions. It is
good to break
something once in
a while. You will
learn the properties
and limits of
materials faster in
this way.

Hole

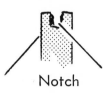

Notch

Tape

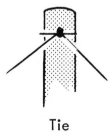

Tie

CHANGE THE WEIGHT

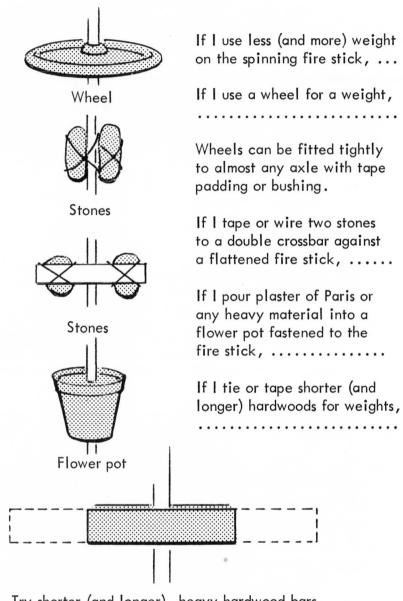

Wheel

If I use less (and more) weight on the spinning fire stick, ...

If I use a wheel for a weight,

. . . .

Stones

Wheels can be fitted tightly to almost any axle with tape padding or bushing.

If I tape or wire two stones to a double crossbar against a flattened fire stick, ...

Stones

If I pour plaster of Paris or any heavy material into a flower pot fastened to the fire stick, ...

Flower pot

If I tie or tape shorter (and longer) hardwoods for weights,

. . . .

Try shorter (and longer), heavy hardwood bars

USE A GUN DRILL FOR CONTROL

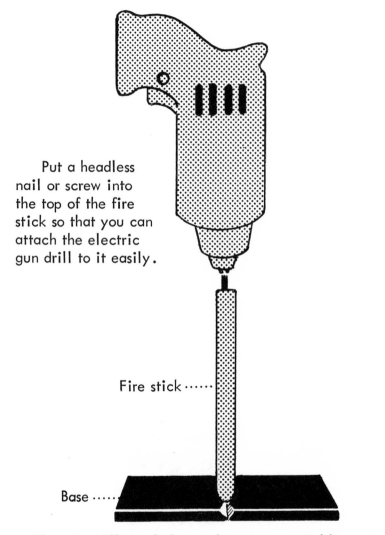

Put a headless nail or screw into the top of the fire stick so that you can attach the electric gun drill to it easily.

Fire stick ......

Base ......

The gun drill can help you keep your variables under control so that you will know which condition caused the difference in which you are interested.

CHANGE THE AIR

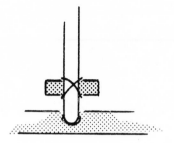

Fan on fire stick

Fresh air with oxygen is the most important thing you need to make a fire with the fire bow. Don't give up easily when you get a little tired. You are very close to making fire when you see smoke.

If I tie or tape a fan to the bottom of my fire stick, ...

If I put a propeller on the fire stick to blow fresh air downward, ...

If I use a ventilating fan or a vacuum cleaner to clear away the smoke and fumes and to bring in fresh air with oxygen, ...

If I blow with a tube to specific glowing spots in my charred sawdust, ...

If I use an empty, plastic squirt bottle for a bellows, ...

Blow on the hot spot

COMPETITIONS WITH THE FIRE BOW

You probably have agreed by now that this challenge to make fire with the fire bow is the hardest problem presented in this book. But, if you have been successful, you are feeling very proud of yourself. The kinds of competition which are commonly seen in adventure programs, survival classes, and science clubs are:

Who can char the end of the fire stick most quickly?

Who can make smoke most quickly?

Who can produce the first red spark?

Who can make fire most quickly?

Encourage team participation because you will get so interested that you will not realize how tired you are getting. Relays are fun, and they will give you rest periods which you will appreciate. The first person on each team makes smoke (a spark or a fire) which activates the second team member. The activity is usually relayed through three or four team members.

A relay team in action

FIRE BOW BIBLIOGRAPHY

The origin of fire making is discussed in most ancient history books. However, most of them are hard for young people to read. Here are three books which have been written especially for young readers:

Henry	Fire
Holden	All About Fire
Hough	Story of Fire

Look up key words in the reference books like: fire, friction, fire making, fire bow, fire drill, hand drill, palm drill, fire plough or plow, fire ball, tinder, and kindling temperature. Here are four good articles to get you started:

Book of Popular Science, 1968, Volume 4, pages 17-18

Compton's Encyclopedia, 1974, Volume 9, page 122

Merit Students' Encyclopedia, 1976, Volume 7, pages 45-46

World Book Encyclopedia, 1976, Volume 7, pages 116-118

SUGGESTIONS FOR TEACHERS

Science homework can be enjoyable and challenging. This is a wonderful time for developing independence and creative skills. The best teaching has taken place when learners keep on trying enthusiastically when working by themselves.

A Ditto-printed challenge can be offered on Monday morning. Hard-to-obtain materials can be distributed so that each student can have a fair chance to get started. Sometimes a related warm-up problem is presented in class to give students the feel of the new materials with which they will be working. An oral discussion might be initiated inviting students to think of experiments which they could do at home. Be sure that all students are able to get a good start.

Then students are on their own initiative during the week to develop solutions to the problem at home. The younger students should not be asked to keep a record of their experimenting. Older students can do this easily.

On Friday the experimental fun comes to a climax. By this time mental models have been converted into physical models. These are brought to school, and contests, competitions, and tournaments decide who has solved the problem best. Many students have asked that this be their testing procedure in science because, they say, one should be given more credit for being able to do something rather than for just being able to talk or to write about it. Teachers respond happily to this idea because it can eliminate much subjective, time-consuming interpretation of student work for grading.

INDEX

INDEX

THE AUTHOR

Al G. Renner has spent
most of his teaching career
either teaching science
or teaching teachers
to teach science. He has
been a science consultant
to many school systems
in Southern California.

Mr. Renner was born in
Montana, but he has lived
most of his life in California.
At the present time he is
teaching science at the
Polytechnic School in Pasadena.

13301

500.028 Renner, Al G.
REN

How to build a
better mousetrap
car--and other
experimental
science fun

DATE			
FE 15 '79			
FE 24 '82			

© THE BAKER & TAYLOR CO.